P9-CLR-377

# Improving Workplace Performance Through Coaching

## Karen Lawson, Ph.D.

**American Media Publishing**
4900 University Avenue
West Des Moines, IA 50266-6769
800-262-2557

# Improving Workplace Performance Through Coaching

Karen Lawson, Ph.D.
Copyright 1996 by Karen Lawson, Ph.D.

**Credits:**

| | |
|---|---|
| American Media Publishing: | Arthur Bauer |
| | Todd McDonald |
| Managing Editor: | Karen Massetti Miller |
| Designer: | Gayle O'Brien |

Published by American Media Inc., 4900 University Avenue, West Des Moines, IA 50266-6769

**Library of Congress Card Number 96-079982**
**Lawson, Karen**
*Improving Workplace Performance Through Coaching*

Printed in the United States of America
ISBN 1-884926-39-8

# Introduction

Coaching is a critical skill for today's manager. Why is coaching so important? Today's environment has created pressure to do more with less. The key to reducing that pressure is to make the most of your most valuable resource—people. The goal of this book is to help managers, supervisors, and coworkers coach employees to overcome barriers and improve performance. This innovative approach to solving performance problems presents a coaching model and creative coaching techniques that will help managers create a supportive environment and address individual differences, including language, culture, age, and value systems.

# About the Author

Karen Lawson, Ph.D., international consultant, speaker, and writer, is president of Lawson Consulting Group, a Philadelphia-based firm specializing in organizational and management development. Dr. Lawson has extensive consulting and workshop experience in the areas of team development, communication, management, and quality service. She has conducted public workshops for colleges and universities as well as trade associations and has been a speaker at many professional conferences. Her clients include a variety of prominent organizations from industry, financial services, health care, retail, government, and education.

Dr. Lawson holds a doctorate in Adult and Organizational Development from Temple University. She is active in many professional organizations. She is past president of the Philadelphia-Delaware Valley Chapter of the American Society for Training and Development (ASTD) and was director of the ASTD National Executive Committee of the Sales and Marketing Professional Practice Area. She is also a past president of the Liberty Bell Chapter of the National Speakers Association. She is author of *The Art of Influencing* and the coauthor of *101 Ways to Make Training Active*. She was an editor for and contributor to *Twenty Active Training Programs, Volume II* and has published dozens of articles in professional journals.

# Contents

# Self-Assessment: How Do I Rate as a Coach?

This self-assessment will help you identify those areas where you can improve as a coach. Remember that your goal is to enhance your existing coaching skills so that you can help your employees be more effective in their jobs.

| *To what degree do I . . .* | Small Degree | | | Large Degree | | |
|---|---|---|---|---|---|---|
| 1. Set specific performance standards and expectations for my employees? | 1 | 2 | 3 | 4 | 5 | 6 |
| 2. Help employees set their own goals? | 1 | 2 | 3 | 4 | 5 | 6 |
| 3. Carefully plan for a coaching session by determining what I want to say and what I want the outcome to be? | 1 | 2 | 3 | 4 | 5 | 6 |
| 4. Address specific behavior rather than attitude or evaluative judgments? | 1 | 2 | 3 | 4 | 5 | 6 |
| 5. Begin a coaching session by expressing empathy and understanding? | 1 | 2 | 3 | 4 | 5 | 6 |
| 6. Use active listening techniques such as paraphrase or restatement to ensure clear understanding between myself and my employee? | 1 | 2 | 3 | 4 | 5 | 6 |
| 7. Give the employee opportunities to offer suggestions? | 1 | 2 | 3 | 4 | 5 | 6 |
| 8. Use open-ended questions to encourage employees to open up and express themselves? | 1 | 2 | 3 | 4 | 5 | 6 |
| 9. Demonstrate support by using praise and agreement to reinforce what the employee says? | 1 | 2 | 3 | 4 | 5 | 6 |

|     |                                                                                          | **Small Degree** |   |   | **Large Degree** |   |   |
| --- | ---------------------------------------------------------------------------------------- | --- | --- | --- | --- | --- | --- |
| 10. | Create an open environment that encourages collaborative, two-way communication?         | 1 | 2 | 3 | 4 | 5 | 6 |
| 11. | Guide employees in a problem-solving process rather than tell them what to do?            | 1 | 2 | 3 | 4 | 5 | 6 |
| 12. | Help employees develop a performance improvement plan?                                    | 1 | 2 | 3 | 4 | 5 | 6 |
| 13. | Meet regularly with employees to monitor their performance improvement efforts?           | 1 | 2 | 3 | 4 | 5 | 6 |
| 14. | Reward employees for achieving the desired results?                                       | 1 | 2 | 3 | 4 | 5 | 6 |
| 15. | Explain how what they do fits into the "big picture"?                                     | 1 | 2 | 3 | 4 | 5 | 6 |
| 16. | Communicate to my employees that I have confidence in them and their abilities?           | 1 | 2 | 3 | 4 | 5 | 6 |
| 17. | Prioritize areas for improvement rather than address everything at once?                  | 1 | 2 | 3 | 4 | 5 | 6 |
| 18. | View coaching as one of my most important managerial responsibilities?                    | 1 | 2 | 3 | 4 | 5 | 6 |
| 19. | Show a genuine interest in the employees during a coaching session through positive, nonverbal behavior? | 1 | 2 | 3 | 4 | 5 | 6 |
| 20. | Give positive reinforcement to an employee for improving performance, even if the employee has not yet met my expectations? | 1 | 2 | 3 | 4 | 5 | 6 |

Use the following scale to determine your success as a coach:

| | |
| --- | --- |
| 101—120 | You are a top-notch, supportive performance coach. |
| 81—100 | Your coaching skills need some fine-tuning. |
| 61—80 | You need to focus on a few areas for improvement. |
| 41—60 | Coaching skills improvement needs to be a top priority. |
| 0—40 | You need to closely examine your basic management practices. |

# What Is Coaching?

**A**s organizations continue to reorganize and reengineer, our workforce will become increasingly empowered and self-directed. Employees will no longer be satisfied with receiving information on a need-to-know basis. They will want to know what the organization's plan is, how they fit into that plan, and whether their performance is meeting organizational goals. To meet these needs, the manager's role must change, too, from the traditional task-assigner to that of a coach and facilitator.

In Part I, we will look at exactly what coaching is, when it should be used, and how it can be supported through employee motivation. In Part II, we'll take a step-by-step look at the coaching process.

# From Boss to Coach

## Chapter Objectives:

☑ Identify the benefits of coaching.

☑ Distinguish between *coaching, counseling,* and *training* and the situations in which they should be used.

☑ Identify the characteristics and skills of effective coaches.

**In today's organization, coaching is an integral part of the overall performance-management system.**

Although we recognize and value the coach's role in the sports arena, we often fail to transfer the principles and practices of coaching to the corporate "playing field." But in today's organization, coaching is an integral part of the overall performance-management system.

In the past, organizations conducted once-a-year performance appraisals and issued evaluations that were similar to school report cards. But this approach doesn't provide employees with the ongoing feedback they need to succeed in today's fast-paced workplace.

Today's managers can't stop at simply evaluating performance—they need to manage it. That means providing employees with information about performance issues as they occur rather than just once a year. The purpose of coaching in these situations is to improve that performance. And, in some cases, coaching becomes one of the first steps in the process of progressive discipline.

Besides improving performance, coaching can also have a positive effect on employee morale. Managers today sometimes have difficulty motivating their employees. Many have discovered that coaching is an effective approach to increasing productivity and improving employee job satisfaction.

## Take a Moment

The first step in moving from being a "boss" to a "coach" is to change your mindset. Using the following T-chart, list the words you associate with the word *boss* and the words you associate with the word *coach*.

| Boss | Coach |
| --- | --- |
| _____ | _____ |
| _____ | _____ |
| _____ | _____ |
| _____ | _____ |
| _____ | _____ |

# Bosses and Coaches: Different Approaches

To illustrate the difference between a traditional boss and a coach, consider the following situation:

*John has been with the organization for eight years and in the same position for five of those years. He is a good employee who does his job and is solid, honest, and reliable. Although he meets standards and expectations, including deadlines, John shows no initiative and resists new ideas and new ways of doing things.*

In dealing with John, a traditional boss might simply ignore the situation, assuming that John is perfectly happy with his job and just wants to keep plugging along. At most, a traditional manager might talk to John and tell him that he should try new ideas and new approaches.

In contrast, a coach recognizes John's potential and takes the time to sit down with John and find out what he likes about his job and what he might like to do to enhance it. A coach will express confidence in John's ability to excel and encourage him to seek additional opportunities.

# What Is Coaching?

**Coaching is an ongoing process designed to help the employee gain greater competence.**

Coaching is an ongoing process designed to help the employee gain greater competence and overcome barriers to improving performance. Coaching is appropriate when an employee has the ability and knowledge to succeed but performance is not at the level needed. The goal of coaching is to create a change in behavior, to move employees from where they are to where you want them to be. Coaching encourages people to do more than they ever imagined they could.

## Two Types of Coaching

There are two different types of coaching: spontaneous, on-the-spot coaching and planned, formal coaching. Both can be effective if done properly; however, many attempts at on-the-spot coaching fail because of the manager's natural tendency to take over. For example, a manager who accompanies a sales rep on a call may intervene to "save" the sale if she sees the call is going badly. Instead, the manager could allow the employee to deal with the situation and then coach the employee afterward. Another manager may believe he is coaching when he pushes an employee away from the computer and says, "Here, let me show you," and then finishes the job.

These interventions are not coaching—they demonstrate a lack of confidence in the employee and undermine any further coaching efforts. Good coaching, whether planned or spontaneous, focuses on developing the employee, not making the manager look good.

# Coaching Versus Training and Counseling

Coaching differs from training, which is a structured process that provides employees with the knowledge and skills to perform job tasks. Coaching also differs from counseling, which is directed at personal issues that are affecting (or have the potential to affect) performance. Very often, counseling involves personal problems, such as marital and family problems, substance abuse, and emotional and psychological barriers. The manager should not try to counsel but should serve as a resource person, directing the employee to a skilled practitioner for further professional help.

## Situations That Require . . .

### Training
- Change in procedures
- New tools or equipment
- New responsibilities
- Move to new department

### Coaching
- Increase in errors
- Missed deadlines
- Meeting only minimum standards
- Untapped potential
- Ability to do better
- Need to fine-tune skills

### Counseling
- Chronic tardiness or absenteeism
- Emotional outbursts
- Erratic behavior
- Suspected substance abuse

## Take a Moment

Identify an employee whose performance you would like to improve through coaching. You will work with this example as you move through the book.

Name:

_____

_____

Situation:

_____

_____

That's enough for now; we'll return to this employee frequently as we move through the book.

# Benefits of Coaching

**Coaching is the most effective way to develop your employees.**

Though coaching employees will take a commitment of your time and effort, it will provide benefits for you as well as your employees.

■ Coaching is the most effective way to develop your employees. The time you invest will produce long-lasting results.

■ Coaching is the key to managing multiple priorities. In today's world of downsizing, cost-cutting, and reengineering, managers are expected to do more with less. High-performing employees, developed through coaching, will help reduce the stress of increasing responsibilities and multiple tasks.

■ Coaching leads to improved employee performance, which leads to increased productivity and bottom-line results. When your employees meet or exceed expectations, everybody wins—you, your employees, and the organization.

■ Coaching increases employees' self-esteem and job satisfaction. People perform better when they feel good about who they are and what they do.

Another reason for learning how to coach is that employees demand it. Today's employees are not content with just being told what to do. They expect their managers to provide them with the tools, techniques, and coaching that will enable them to excel.

# Barriers to Coaching

If coaching is such a great approach, why don't more managers practice it? The primary barrier to effective coaching can be found within managers and employees themselves. Reasons why some managers are poor coaches include:

■ They don't know how to coach. Many managers are promoted to their positions because they were good at what they did, but are left to develop their management techniques through trial and error or modeling the behavior of other managers. If they were never coached along the way, they won't know how to do it. This barrier to coaching can be overcome by a variety of training resources, such as this book.

■ They don't want to take the time to coach. No doubt about it, coaching takes time, and that's something most managers are short on. But taking the time to coach can save managers more time later on. Time management experts have found that for every hour spent planning, three to four hours are saved in execution. The same principle holds true for coaching. Time spent coaching in the short term results in long-term benefits.

■ They don't have the patience to coach. Some people simply are not patient by nature. But even the most impatient person can develop patience by focusing on the positive outcomes of coaching and practicing it on a daily basis.

■ They believe employees should improve performance on their own. Many managers believe that once an employee is selected for a job, performance improvement is his or her responsibility—a case of "sink or swim." In some cases, the manager may think "I had to learn it the hard way, and if I can do it, so can everyone else." These managers need to remember that trial and error is a very inefficient teacher. Employees will perform better and be more productive if managers take the time to coach.

> **The primary barrier to effective coaching can be found within managers and employees themselves.**

Of course, managers aren't the only barrier to effective coaching. Employees themselves are often the problem. No matter how skillful or committed the coach may be, coaching cannot succeed unless the employee is "coachable." Reasons employees might be difficult to coach include:

■ They are resistant to change. Coaching requires that employees change their behavior, and many people are uncomfortable with change. Some employees may be so entrenched in their current behavior that they see change—and coaching—as a personal threat.

■ They think they know it all. Overconfidence sometimes creates a know-it-all attitude. Employees who think they have all the answers will see no reason to change their behaviors and will initially resist coaching efforts.

Though employees with these attitudes may be difficult to deal with, coaches can overcome both types of employee objections to coaching by carefully explaining the reasons why a behavior change is necessary and describing how the employee will benefit from it.

# Criteria for Success

**Successful coaches know how to bring out the best in others and have a desire to participate actively in each employee's development.**

Successful coaches in business, as in sports, are great influencers. They know how to bring out the best in others and have a desire to participate actively in each employee's development. They also know that coaching is an ongoing process and a primary responsibility. They create an environment that empowers groups and individuals to get results.

Being a good coach is a challenge, but it is a challenge that managers can meet if they develop the appropriate qualities, characteristics, and skills and translate those into effective coaching behaviors.

## Take a Moment

Identify three situations in which you received effective coaching from someone. These examples can be taken from any time in your life and any type of situation, personal or professional.

Example #1:

Example #2:

Example #3:

Based on these three examples, list below the qualities, characteristics, or skills below that you think an effective coach must have.

1._____   6._____
2._____   7._____
3._____   8._____
4._____   9._____
5._____   10._____

# Characteristics and Skills of Effective Coaches

Studies show that effective coaches share certain personal characteristics, including:

■ *Patience*—Successful coaches discipline themselves to be patient and understanding. They realize that behavior change takes time and performance improvement happens incrementally.

■ *Enthusiasm*—All good coaches are enthusiastic, and they show it. If you have any doubts, just watch the sidelines at a football or basketball game. The coaches are excited, and their enthusiasm becomes contagious. Imagine the results if the great Vince Lombardi had said to his team in a matter-of-fact tone: "Well, you know, guys, it's your job to get out there and win. Give it your best shot."

**Successful coaches truly care about people.**

- *Honesty and integrity*—Effective coaches are noted for their forthrightness and high principles. People follow them because they do the right thing.

- *Friendliness*—To be a successful coach, you need to draw people to you. An unfriendly demeanor will discourage others from seeking your help or from receiving your coaching efforts.

- *Genuine concern for others*—Successful coaches truly care about people and demonstrate their concern through words and deeds.

- *Self-confidence*—To be able to coach others successfully, you have to have confidence in yourself, believing that you know what you're doing and can offer sound guidance to others.

- *Fairness*—The ability to treat people fairly is a quality that goes a long way to engender loyalty and trust from people around you. How often have you thought about a manager or even a teacher you had who was "tough but fair"? That's probably the person from whom you learned the most and certainly the one you most respect.

- *Consistency*—Moodiness or mercurial behavior will sabotage your success as a coach, no matter how good you may be at the coaching process. People need to know that you are consistent in your expectations of them as well as of yourself.

- *Flexibility*—It's been said that managers do things right, and leaders do the right thing. Doing the right thing in the right situation means that you have to be flexible and use your judgment in making a decision or adapting your coaching style to the individual and the situation.

- *Resourcefulness*—Good coaches know how to get things done. They have the ability to draw on a variety of resources to aid in the coaching process. If they don't know the answer, they know whom to ask or where to go for help.

- *Empathy*—Good coaches have the ability to put themselves in the other person's shoes. They remember what it was like to learn a new task. Or they know what it means to feel inadequate in certain aspects of the job.

In addition to these qualities and characteristics, coaches need to develop the following skills and abilities:

- Communicating effectively

- Listening

- Questioning

- Setting goals and objectives

- Establishing appropriate priorities

- Analyzing

- Planning and organizing

We will address these skills as we look at the coaching process step by step.

## Take a Moment

Go back over the list of qualities and skills and highlight those you believe you already have. Then identify those you would like to develop further.

■ Qualities and skills I already have:

_____

_____

_____

_____

■ Qualities and skills I would like to develop:

_____

_____

_____

_____

**You can use the acronym COACH as a handy way to remember some of the most important coaching behaviors.**

# Modeling Coaching Behavior

In addition to characteristics and skills, effective coaches need to demonstrate certain behaviors. You can use the acronym COACH as a handy way to remember some of the most important behaviors: Collaborate, Own, Acknowledge, Communicate, and Help. As we review the behaviors in detail, try to relate each one to yourself and your own situation.

- *Collaborate*—The coaching relationship is a collaborative one. Work with the employee to identify the performance problem, set standards and performance objectives, and develop a performance-improvement plan. Good coaches think in terms of how WE solve the problem.

- *Own*—Examine your own behavior and accept some ownership for the problem. Along with the employee, ask yourself: "Did I make my expectations clear?" "Did I provide the proper training?" "Does the employee have the appropriate tools to do the job?"

- *Acknowledge*—Acknowledge employee achievements as well as problems, feelings, and concerns. The last point can be a challenge. Acknowledging problems and concerns is not the same as overlooking them or excusing unacceptable behavior or performance. For example, you can certainly acknowledge an employee's difficulty in juggling the multiple responsibilities of both home and work. However, you cannot accept the resulting chronic absenteeism or tardiness.

- *Communicate*—This is probably the most important behavior and the one many managers seem to find the most difficult. As we noted earlier, communication skills, including listening, questioning, and giving and receiving feedback are critical for success. Coaches need to practice two-way communication on a daily basis and clarify expectations regularly.

- *Help*—As a manager, you are not only a coach but also an advisor, serving as a resource person and a guide to other resources, both inside and outside the organization. In addition to giving help, you should also be seeking help from your employees. For example, if you need to increase sales, ask your employees to help you develop a marketing plan. At the very least, solicit your employees' ideas. You will be surprised at how creative and innovative people can be when you give them a chance.

**Making the change from traditional manager to coach will require a commitment of your time and energy.**

# The Coaching Challenge

Making the change from traditional manager to coach will require a commitment of your time and energy as you develop new qualities, skills, and behaviors and improve communication with your employees. However, the benefits you and your staff will enjoy in improved performance, morale, and productivity will make your investment a worthwhile one.

# Chapter One Review

Answers may be found on page 92.

1. True or False?
   An annual performance appraisal can take the place of regular coaching.

2. Match the situations below with the type of treatment they require:
   a. Coaching
   b. Training
   c. Counseling
   ___ Chronic tardiness or absenteeism
   ___ Meeting only minimum standards
   ___ New responsibilities

3. List four reasons why managers can be poor coaches.
   _____
   _____
   _____
   _____

4. List two reasons why employees may be uncoachable.
   _____
   _____

5. Which of the following is *not* a characteristic of good coaches?
   a. Enthusiasm
   b. Placing results above all other concerns
   c. Honesty and integrity
   d. Self-confidence

6. List three behaviors that good coaches demonstrate.
   _____
   _____
   _____

# Understanding Today's Employee

## Chapter Objectives:

 Describe the manager's role as a coach and motivator.

 Identify different approaches to motivating today's employees.

Even the best coach can't force a team member or employee to change his or her behavior—the motivation to change has to come from within the individual. But coaches/managers can create an environment that fosters motivation by helping employees see the WIIFT of behavior change: What's in It for Them. To do this effectively, managers need to understand the nature of motivation and what employees hope to get from their work.

# What Employees Want

**Effective managers motivate their employees by offering them a variety of incentives and rewards.**

Motivation is directly related to morale, that is, the attitude of individuals and groups toward their work, work environment, and the organization as a whole. Effective managers motivate their employees by offering them a variety of incentives and rewards. Researchers often divide these into two categories:

■ Maintainers

■ Motivators

Maintainers are factors that must be kept at a satisfactory level in order for employees to maintain performance. They include the following:

■ Working conditions

■ Company policies

■ Job security

■ Pay and benefits

■ Relationships with coworkers

■ Supervision

■ Status

**Does your organization provide incentives that will motivate employees to make changes you want them to make?**

True motivators are the factors that create an inner desire to work by satisfying certain needs that are important to the individual. They include:

■ Achievement

■ Recognition

■ Satisfying work

■ Responsibility

■ Advancement

■ Growth

Before you begin to coach your employees, analyze your organization based on these two categories. Does it provide incentives that will motivate employees to make the changes you want them to make? If not, what can you do to improve the situation and create a positive motivational climate?

## Managers and Employees: Different Perceptions

The list on the previous page suggest a number of rewards that managers may offer employees in order to maintain and improve performance. Yet managers very often misinterpret what their employees want and attempt to motivate them with rewards that the employees simply do not value.

### Take a Moment

Take a moment and rank order the following motivating factors according to what is important to you.

- Full appreciation of work done
- Feeling of being in on things
- Sympathetic help with personal problems
- Job security
- Good wages
- Interesting work
- Promotion and growth in the organization
- Personal loyalty to employees
- Good working conditions
- Tactful discipline

Now go back over the list and identify the order you think your employees would choose.

Over the past 50 years, several studies have been conducted in which employees were asked to rank ten rewards in terms of their importance or motivational value to them.

- Full appreciation of work done

- Feeling of being in on things

- Sympathetic help on personal problems

- Job security

- Good wages

- Interesting work

- Promotion and growth in the organization

- Personal loyalty to employees

- Good working conditions

- Tactful discipline

After the employees rank-ordered the rewards, their supervisors were asked to rank the same items according to how they thought their employees would rank them. The first study was conducted in 1946, the second in 1981, and the most recent in 1995. In all three cases, what managers and supervisors thought was important to employees differed dramatically from what employees said was important to them.

In each study, employees ranked job security and good wages near the middle, yet supervisors believed their employees would put good wages and job security in slots one and two, respectively. In fact, in the 1995 study conducted by Kenneth Kovack at George Mason University, supervisor and employee ranking looks like this:

| Motivating Factors | Supervisor | Employee |
|---|---|---|
| • Full appreciation of work done | 8 | 2 |
| • Feeling of being in on things | 10 | 3 |
| • Help on personal problems | 9 | 10 |
| • Job security | 2 | 4 |
| • Good wages | 1 | 5 |
| • Interesting work | 5 | 1 |
| • Promotion and growth | 3 | 6 |
| • Loyalty from boss | 6 | 8 |
| • Working conditions | 4 | 7 |
| • Tactful disciplining | 7 | 9 |

Notice that supervisors put *feeling of being in on things* as number ten, and employees rank it among the top three!

These studies show that managers are often totally wrong in predicting how their employees would rank the list. What are the implications for coaching? If managers misinterpret what is important to their employees, they will choose methods of motivation that are entirely off-base. For example, a manager may believe that all employees are motivated primarily by money, so she uses a bonus as an incentive for improved performance. Much to her surprise, employee performance does not improve. What the manager does not realize is that there may be other factors that are more important to her employees.

> **If managers misinterpret what is important to their employees, they will choose methods of motivation that are entirely off-base.**

Based on the above study, the manager in our example would have better luck if she tried a different approach. She should learn what her employees hope to accomplish on the job so that she can provide them with *interesting work.* She should express *full appreciation* for the work they do, especially when performance improves, and she should keep employees informed of what's going on in the organization so that they feel that they are *in on things.*

How can you find out what will motivate your employees to change behavior in a coaching situation? You could ask them to complete the above assessment, but you might not get accurate data. The best way is to talk to your employees and really listen to them. They will let you know directly or indirectly what's important to them. For example, if you have an employee who frequently asks you, "How am I doing?" or "Did you like the way I handled that situation?" that's a good indication the employee is motivated by recognition.

# Motivating Different Age Groups

> **Motivating employees is complicated further by generational differences.**

Motivating employees is complicated further by generational differences. More than ever before, today's managers find themselves managing several generations of people at once, and the factors that motivate each group differ considerably. For example, people born roughly between 1943 and 1960 have been influenced by the events of the '60s and '70s. Idealistic and moralistic, the baby boomers' primary motivators have been money and freedom. Those born between 1920 and 1942 were impacted by the Great Depression and believe strongly in the importance of security and loyalty.

The so-called "Generation X" (born during the years 1965 to 1979), who were raised on computers, video games, and VCRs, are both realistic and cynical. They have grown up watching their "workaholic" parents spend 14 to 16 hours at the office, foregoing family vacations, only to find themselves tossed out after 25 years of loyal service to the company. Forget loyalty—Generation Xers want what they want now. They're interested in rewarding challenges and are willing to work hard, yet unlike their parents, they fiercely guard their personal and leisure time. Because many grew up in dual career or single-parent families, they are self-reliant and independent and are not as intimidated by authority figures as those in previous generations.

## Take a Moment

Think about your employees who represent different generations. How does what motivates them differ? How do they say or communicate what is important to them?

_____

_____

_____

# Creating a Supportive Work Environment

**Studies show that when managers create a supportive, nurturing climate, people do what they believe is expected of them.**

With so many different factors affecting employee motivation, where does a manager begin? Creating a supportive environment is a good first step. Studies show that when managers create a supportive, nurturing climate, people do what they believe is expected of them. Managers can create such a climate in several ways:

■ Expect the best from employees.

■ Develop a flexible management style.

■ Eliminate barriers to individual achievement.

## Expect the Best

**What a manager expects of team members, combined with the way he or she treats them, will help determine the success or failure of those people.**

When managers create high performance expectations and communicate them, team members work to meet them.

People of all ages want to do a good job. Children start school eager and enthusiastic, yet within a relatively short period of time, much of that exuberance fades. Employees bring the same positive attitude and motivation to the workplace. Have you ever heard anyone say, "I'm going to go to work today and do a bad job"?

What a manager expects of team members, combined with the way he or she treats them, will help determine the success or failure of those people. In their landmark book *In Search of Excellence*, authors Peters and Waterman put it very succinctly: "Label a man a loser, and he'll start acting like one."

## Take a Moment

List four situations or people in your workplace that would require you to modify your management style. Next to each name, write how you would change your style when working with that person or situation.

1._____/_____
2._____/_____
3._____/_____
4._____/_____

## Develop a Flexible Management Style

How would you characterize your management style? Do you use the same approach in every situation? Many managers pride themselves on treating everyone the same, but doing so can be dangerous. Employees are individuals with individual needs. Managers should treat everyone fairly, but not necessarily the same.

Managing flexibly also means varying your approach not only to the individual but also to the situation. An employee who is new to the job will need more direction than a five-year veteran. However, if the veteran employee is given a new task or responsibility, that person may need more direction in that particular situation.

## Eliminate Barriers to Individual Achievement

Identify an employee who is not performing as you would like. Ask yourself if there is a barrier to that person's achievement that you have not previously considered. Many people who are labeled "failures" or "incompetents" are simply being hindered by relatively minor obstacles that managers have not recognized. The tragedy is that after a while, the employee may begin to accept the failure label as fact.

When confronted with an employee who is not working up to standard, ask yourself: Does the employee have the knowledge and skills to do the job? If not, it's your job to provide him or her with the necessary training. Does the person have the appropriate tools? If not, get them. Make sure people have the training, information, tools, and equipment to do the job.

# Reward, Recognition, and Reinforcement

Reward, recognition, and reinforcement go hand-in-hand with motivation, but many managers still use old-fashioned, ineffective methods of rewarding employees. Some managers try to inspire achievement with the carrot-on-the-stick approach, using incentive programs, promises of rewards, and bonuses. Others penalize negative behavior by wielding the symbolic whip. This type of manager might say, "If you don't start getting to work on time, you'll be fired," or "You'll never get ahead if you continue to make these kinds of mistakes."

The problem with these methods is that they are short-term. Such quick fixes create no permanent behavior change. The next time, instead of a whip, the manager will have to use a symbolic club to correct the employee, or the carrot that's being dangled will have to get bigger.

Rather than dangling carrots or wielding clubs, managers' efforts are much more successful if they think of reward and recognition in terms of a flowering plant. In order to get a plant to bloom, you must create the appropriate environment using the right amount of light, water, temperature, and fertilizer. And if you have different types of plants, each will require different care. People are similar. The most successful rewards systems make allowances for individual differences.

**Simply offering encouragement is an important first step in the recognition process.**

Simply offering encouragement is an important first step in the recognition process. Managers can develop a sense of competence and confidence in others by encouraging them to stretch, to acknowledge their own accomplishments, and to strive toward their personal best. Point out improvements in performance, no matter how small. This is particularly important when employees are beginning new tasks. As Goethe once said, "Correction does much, but encouragement more; encouragement after censure is as the sun after a shower."

Encouragement and reinforcement need to be followed with recognition and rewards. Individual recognition teamed with incentive programs can be very effective, but should be tied to organizational goals and consist of something that will be valued by the employee. If, for example, your organization is committed to responding quickly to customers, then you should reward employee efficiency in returning phone calls or resolving complaints.

Any reward should be tailored to the person receiving it. The employee with young children may appreciate being given more scheduling flexibility, while someone on a limited income would value the opportunity to work overtime. Other reward possibilities include public recognition, vacations, or tangibles such as gifts or tickets to the theater or an athletic event.

# Inspiring Employees to Change

**Learn what motivates your employees and what types of rewards and recognition they value.**

There are many ways that coaches/managers can create a workplace in which employees will be motivated to make behavioral changes, and there are many ways in which managers can reward employees for their efforts. The secret to success is to learn what motivates your employees and what types of rewards and recognition they value. Listen to your employees; learn about their preferences and what they hope to gain from their work. Then create an environment in which each one can reach his or her highest potential.

# Chapter Two Review

Answers appear on pages 92 and 93.

1. List three maintainers and three motivators:

   _____

   _____

   _____

   _____

   _____

   _____

2. True or False?
   In several studies, employees ranked *feeling of being in on things* as one of the top three things they wanted from their jobs.

3. True or False?
   Today's younger workers want pretty much what their parents and grandparents wanted from their jobs.

4. List three factors that can help a manager create a supportive work environment.

   _____

   _____

   _____

5. True or False?
   Different employees require different types of rewards and recognition.

# PART II

# The Coaching Process

**W**e have seen what coaching is and how employee motivation is necessary for coaching to succeed. We will now look at the steps of the coaching process.

The coaching process can be broken into three main segments:

■ Planning and preparation

■ Conducting the coaching session

■ Action-planning and follow-up

Within each part are a number of individual steps, as illustrated by the flowchart in Figure 1.

We will consider each of those steps and the skills necessary to successfully complete them in chapters 3–6. In chapter 7, you will have the opportunity to create an action plan to develop your own coaching skills.

# The Coaching Process

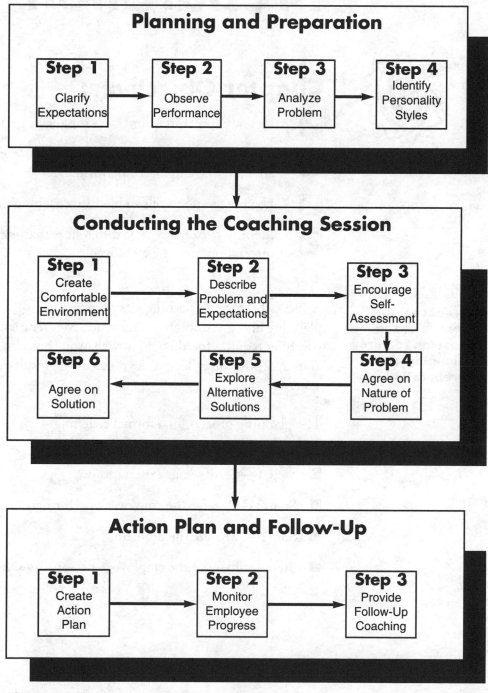

**Planning and Preparation**

**Step 1** Clarify Expectations → **Step 2** Observe Performance → **Step 3** Analyze Problem → **Step 4** Identify Personality Styles

**Conducting the Coaching Session**

**Step 1** Create Comfortable Environment → **Step 2** Describe Problem and Expectations → **Step 3** Encourage Self-Assessment

**Step 6** Agree on Solution ← **Step 5** Explore Alternative Solutions ← **Step 4** Agree on Nature of Problem

**Action Plan and Follow-Up**

**Step 1** Create Action Plan → **Step 2** Monitor Employee Progress → **Step 3** Provide Follow-Up Coaching

**Figure 1**

# Planning and Preparation

## Chapter Objectives:

☑ Define expectations for your employee's performance.

☑ Analyze the work situation to determine what might be affecting the employee's performance.

☑ Use observation skills to identify coaching needs.

☑ Identify personality style differences that may affect your interaction with the employee.

**A successful formal coaching session requires planning and preparation.**

A successful formal coaching session doesn't just happen. It takes planning and preparation—sometimes even rehearsal. Informal coaching requires forethought as well. You should never coach an employee without at least a clear idea of the result you hope to achieve.

The planning process for a formal coaching session consists of four basic steps:

■ **Step 1**—Clarify your expectations.

■ **Step 2**—Observe the employee's performance.

■ **Step 3**—Analyze the problem.

■ **Step 4**—Identify the employee's personality style.

# 1
## Step

**Before you begin to work with the employee, you will need to clarify your expectations for that person's performance.**

# Clarify Expectations

Before you begin to work with the employee, you will need to clarify your expectations for that person's performance. As you consider what you would like the employee to do, you may be tempted to think in terms of attitude or general qualities.

*"I want Lauren to show a more positive attitude."*

*"Chris needs to be better organized."*

But statements like these will not give your employees the information they need to improve performance—what exactly should Lauren do to show a positive attitude?

Instead of focusing on internal qualities like attitude or general tendencies like neatness, state your expectations in terms of behaviors—specific, observable actions that can be measured. For example, if you want an employee to project a positive attitude toward his or her job, identify the behaviors that are a part of that—coming to work on time, greeting customers in a friendly manner, cooperating with other employees, etc. Describe specifically what kind of behavior you want—or don't want—someone in the employee's position to demonstrate.

## Take a Moment

Rewrite the following statements so that they focus on behavior rather than attitude or general qualities.

1. Leslie is incompetent.

_____

2. Vince is sloppy in his work.

_____

3. Tom just isn't interested in his job.

_____

4. Joan is rude to customers.

_____

Take the time to make a list of the performance behaviors you hope the employee will change before you begin your session so that you will be ready to discuss them. Below is a sample list for Sydney, a clerical worker in a law firm who is having trouble with word-processing.

---

**My Expectations for Sidney's Performance**

I would like Sidney's word-processing to be:

■ Completed on time.

■ Free of typing errors.

---

# 2
## Step

**Try to be as objective as possible, focusing on the behaviors that are causing the performance problem, not on your reaction to or evaluation of the situation.**

# Observe Performance

How does the employee's current behavior differ from the behavior you would like to see? To find out, you will need to observe the employee's performance. Try to be as objective as possible, focusing on the behaviors that are causing the performance problem, not on your reaction to or evaluation of the situation. As you record your observations, keep the following guidelines in mind.

■ Focus on specific behaviors that can be measured and changed: *"Jesse was late three times last week."* *"Taylor's production was under quota for the fourth time in a row."*

■ Don't just make note of what the employee is doing wrong. Keep track of what the employee is doing right so that you can build on his or her strengths during the coaching session.

■ Determine the priority of the behaviors that the employee needs to improve. Don't try to work on everything at once; select the behaviors that are most important for the employee's success, and concentrate on those first. You can work on other behaviors in future coaching sessions.

Add your observations of current performance to your previous list of expectations for employee behavior.

**Sidney's Current Performance**
**Last week, I observed that Sidney**

■ Was a day late typing the Smith memo and two days late with the Jennings Report.
■ Had several errors in each of those documents, plus errors in three other documents.

**Aspects of Sidney's behavior I would like to reinforce:**

■ Greeted all visitors with a smile.
■ Was patient with difficult caller.
■ Has set up an effective filing system.

**Priority of behaviors I would like Sidney to improve:**

■ Meet all deadlines.
■ Eliminate errors.

# Take a Moment

Think about the employee you identified in chapter 1. What are your expectations for that person's performance?

_____
_____

What is the person's current behavior? What exactly does the employee do that you want him or her to do differently?

_____
_____

What does the person say or do that you want him or her to continue?

_____
_____

Is there more than one behavior that needs to be changed or improved? If so, rank them in order of importance.

_____
_____

# 3 Step

# Analyze the Problem

As you compare your expectations for an employee's performance to what that person is currently doing, analyze the situation to determine what factors might be affecting the employee's performance and whether coaching is the appropriate solution. You can do this by asking yourself the following questions:

- What aspects of the employee's performance are unsatisfactory? Using your expectations for performance as a benchmark, identify the ways in which the current performance falls short.

- Is it worth my time to coach in this situation? Coaching is an investment of your time as well as the employee's. Does the employee have other problems that will keep him or her from benefiting from the process? Is the performance so poor that full-scale training or counseling is needed?

- Does the employee know my expectations? Does the employee fully understand what is expected of him or her?

**Are extenuating circumstances preventing the employee from doing his or her best?**

- What obstacles are there to meeting those expectations? Are extenuating circumstances preventing the employee from doing his or her best? Possibilities might include lack of proper training, too few resources, unrealistic parameters, or too many other responsibilities.

- What negative or positive consequences follow performance? Does the employee have any motivation to change his or her behavior? What can you do to stimulate that motivation?

- Could the employee change if he or she wanted to? Does the employee have the ability to do the job? After all, "ducks don't climb trees." Do you have a duck in a situation that requires a cat? Sometimes the problem is that we simply have someone in the wrong job. Coaching can't solve all your personnel problems!

As you prepare for your coaching session, prepare a list of answers to these questions, as in the following example:

---

### Analysis of Sidney's Word-Processing Performance:

- **What is unsatisfactory?**
  Sidney's inability to meet deadlines and her high rate of errors. Projects should be error free and on time.

- **Is it worth my time?**
  Yes, Sidney performs her other tasks well.

- **Are my expectations clear?**
  I make deadlines clear to Sidney and point out typing errors.

- **Are there obstacles to meeting them?**
  Sidney has had some training on the word-processing software, but she might need more. I should ask her if she knows how to use the spell-check and macro features and make arrangements for further training if she does not.

- **Consequences of performance?**
  If Sidney's word-processing doesn't improve, she could lose her merit raise.

- **Could Sidney change if she wanted to?**
  Sidney has learned to do new things in the past; she should be able to master the word-processing software.

---

Of course you will need to talk with your employee to learn if your initial assumptions are correct. Keep an open mind as you coach and encourage your employees to share their perspectives with you. You may learn some surprising and useful things about your organization.

## Take a Moment

Think about the employee with a performance problem whom you identified on page 14. Could any of the preceding reasons be the cause of this person's performance problem?

# 4
**Step**

# Identify the Employee's Personality Style

Once you have determined which behaviors you would like to see change and the factors that might be causing the problem, you need to plan how to present this information to the employee. In order to do this effectively, you will need to identify your employee's personality style and adapt your coaching session to that style.

**Our style differences can get in the way of effective coaching because we often relate to the other person in our own style instead of theirs.**

People's personalities can differ in any number of ways; however, psychologists have identified four basic categories of personality styles. Different personality models have given different names to each of the four styles; in this book, we will call them *candid, persuasive, logical,* and *reflective.* Although everyone possesses characteristics from each style, each of us usually has one style that is dominant.

Our style differences can get in the way of effective coaching, because we often relate to the other person in our own style instead of theirs. When that happens, it's almost as though two people are speaking a different language. To increase your coaching effectiveness, you need to adapt your coaching sessions to the personality styles of your employees.

The first step to adapting to your employees' personality styles is to identify your own. Read each of the following sets of questions and check the one in each set that is most like you. After you've read the section on interpreting your score, go back over the questions, and try to imagine how various employees or team members would respond.

**Self-Check**

1. When I am in a learning situation, I like to
___a. Be involved in doing something.
___b. Work with people in groups.
___c. Read about the information.
___d. Watch and listen to what is going on.

2. When I am working in a group, I like to
___a. Direct the discussion and activity.
___b. Find out what other people think and feel.
___c. Remain somewhat detached from the rest of the group.
___d. Go along with the majority.

3. When faced with a conflict situation, I prefer to
___a. Confront the situation head-on and try to win.
___b. Work with the other person to arrive at an amicable resolution.
___c. Present my position by using logic and reason.
___d. Not make waves.

4. In a conversation, I tend to
___a. Come straight to the point.
___b. Draw others into the conversation.
___c. Listen to what others have to say, then offer an objective opinion.
___d. Agree with what others say.

5. When making a decision, I tend to
___a. Make a decision quickly and then move on.
___b. Consider how the outcome will affect others.
___c. Take time to gather facts and data.
___d. Consider all possible outcomes and proceed with caution.

6. I am seen by others as someone who
___a. Gets results.
___b. Is fun to be with.
___c. Is logical and rational.
___d. Is a calming influence.

7. In a work environment, I prefer
___a. To work alone.
___b. To work with others.
___c. Structure and organization.
___d. A peaceful atmosphere.

Now count the number of items checked for each letter. The letter with the most checks indicates your preferred personality style.

a=Candid
b=Persuasive
c=Logical
d=Reflective

As you read the brief descriptions below, determine for yourself the accuracy with which the description reflects your personal style.

# Candid

**Candid individuals like to be both in charge and the center of attention.**

Candid individuals are direct and controlling. They like to be both in charge and the center of attention. They are action-oriented and may be perceived as pushy and domineering. They enjoy being challenged, and they tend to make decisions quickly, sometimes with little information. Those with a candid style are demanding of themselves and others.

To be more effective, the candid person needs to be more sensitive to others, practice active listening, and exercise more caution in making decisions.

You can increase your effectiveness in coaching the candid person by quickly coming to the point during the coaching session. Because the candid person is often a poor listener, you will need to clarify and confirm frequently and ask the employee to summarize the discussion at frequent intervals. It is also important to give the candid employee lots of recognition and reinforcement as well as to challenge him or her with more responsibility and authority.

# Persuasive

**Persuasive people are outgoing, warm, and animated.**

Those whose primary style is persuasive love people. They are outgoing, warm, and animated. They are very sociable and may be perceived as overly emotional. They have a short attention span and dislike details. Persuasive individuals are spontaneous, entertaining, and like to take risks.

To be more effective, the persuasive person needs to improve organization skills and spend more time looking at the facts.

You can increase your effectiveness in coaching the persuasive person by creating a friendly environment. Take time at the beginning of the session to build rapport. Focus on the "people side" of the performance problem and appeal to the employee's concern for others as a motivation for behavioral change.

# Logical

Logical individuals pride themselves on their use of analysis and reason in all situations. They have a strong need to be right, and they rely on facts and data to support their position. Although they are good problem-solvers, they are slow to make decisions. They are sometimes perceived as aloof and critical. They often ask probing questions and frequently take the opposing point of view in a discussion.

To be more effective, the logical person needs to be more flexible, spend less time gathering data, show more concern for people, and be more expressive of his or her feelings.

You can increase your effectiveness in coaching the logical person by using logical analysis to help the employee identify the cause of and the solution to the performance problem. Recognize this person's need for detail and for the reasons behind your suggestions. Present your suggestions in a logical, step-by-step process.

# Reflective

Reflective individuals are reliable and cautious. They tend to be perfectionists and seek security. They avoid conflict and may be perceived by others as weak. Reflective people are good listeners and make great friends. They are loyal, cooperative, and supportive. For this reason, they are good team players.

To be more effective, the reflective person should learn to be more assertive, less sensitive, and more willing to take risks.

You can increase your effectiveness in coaching reflective employees by encouraging and reassuring them. Exercise patience, since reflectives often approach a change in behavior more slowly and cautiously than other types.

Understanding and adjusting to different personality styles will help you become a more effective coach. Your acceptance of others and willingness to adapt will also encourage them to accept and adapt to you as well, creating better relationships throughout your workplace.

# Be Patient

**Formal coaching is never a quick fix—it takes time and patience to facilitate another person's behavior change.**

Formal coaching is never a quick fix—it takes time and patience to facilitate another person's behavior change. As you gain more coaching practice, you will find that what works well for one person may not work for another. You may have to use trial and error until you match the right methods to the right people.

Thorough planning is your first step to making that match. Your next step is to develop your coaching communication, which we will consider in the next two chapters.

# Chapter Three Review

Answers may be found on page 93.

1. In order to coach effectively, you should clarify your expectations for employee behavior (choose one)
   ___ a. At the beginning of the coaching process, before the coaching session begins.
   ___ b. During the coaching session, as you talk to the employee.

2. What are three things on which you should focus when observing employee performance before a coaching session?
   _____
   _____
   _____

3. What are three factors that might cause unsatisfactory performance?
   _____
   _____
   _____

4. Match the following personality styles with their definitions:
   ___ Candid
   ___ Persuasive
   ___ Logical
   ___ Reflective
   a. Uses analysis and reason in all situations.
   b. Outgoing, warm, and animated.
   c. Reliable and cautious; seeks security and avoids conflict.
   d. Direct and controlling; likes to be the center of attention.

# Conducting the Coaching Session:
## Beginning the Session

## Chapter Objectives:

☑    Build rapport with the employee during the coaching session.

☑    Clearly describe the employee's current performance and your expectations for improvement.

☑    Use questioning skills to involve the employee in the coaching process.

☑    Use active listening to ensure two-way collaborative communication.

Once you have fully planned your coaching session, you're ready to conduct it. There are three key steps to beginning a successful coaching session:

■  **Step 1**—Create a comfortable coaching environment.

■  **Step 2**—Describe the performance problem and your expectations for performance.

■  **Step 3**—Encourage employee self-assessment.

# 1
## Step

# Create a Comfortable Coaching Environment

For a coaching session to be effective, the coach needs to create an environment in which the person being coached will feel safe and comfortable. You can do this by:

- Choosing an appropriate time and place for coaching.

- Establishing rapport with the employee.

## Choosing an Appropriate Time and Place

For your coaching session to succeed, both you and the employee should be able to give each other your undivided attention. This often means scheduling a formal coaching session in advance. Whether your coaching session is formal or informal, choose a time when you and your employee are relatively stress-free. To encourage open communication, select a location in which you can sit next to the employee rather than across a desk—this usually means someplace other than your office. Look for a place without a lot of traffic, where you can speak privately. If you will need access to a piece of equipment, such as a computer, be sure it is available.

**Whether your coaching session is formal or informal, choose a time when you and your employee are relatively stress-free.**

## Establishing Rapport

Rather than jumping right in with an evaluation of the employee's performance, begin your coaching session by establishing rapport and clearly stating the purpose for the meeting. For example, after asking the employee how he or she is, you might say something like, "What I would like to discuss with you today is how I can help you be more successful in closing your sales."

Support your friendly approach with nonverbal communication. When the employee speaks, sit forward in your chair to indicate interest, and avoid nervous gestures such as playing with your glasses or tapping your pen. You can inadvertently send out the wrong message by crossing your arms (indicating defensiveness) or leaning back with your hands behind your head and stretching (a demonstration of superiority).

You should not only be conscious of what you are communicating nonverbally but also of what the employee is communicating as well. For example, if an employee is fidgeting in the chair, there's a good chance that he or she is nervous or uncomfortable with the discussion. Look for these cues and do your best to put the employee at ease.

# 2
## Step

**Remember to state the problem in terms of the behaviors you observed rather than trying to evaluate the employee's attitude or emotional state.**

# Describe the Performance Problem

After creating a comfortable climate and putting the employee at ease, you're ready to start the coaching session. Begin by describing the performance problem you identified in your observation of the employee, and compare the employee's current performance to your expectations. Remember to state the problem in terms of the behaviors you observed rather than trying to evaluate the employee's attitude or emotional state.

Your coaching will be most effective if you describe employee performance in precise, objective terms. Use the notes that you took as you observed the employee to help you specify such features as:

- Speed—(rate)

- Quantity—(number or amount)

- Accuracy—(absence of errors)

- Thoroughness—(completeness)

- Timeliness—(ability to meet deadlines)

Here are some examples of coaches who provide specific descriptions of performance problems in relation to expectations:

*"I've noticed that your sales figures have been down for the past six months. The company average is $60,000 per employee, and you've been ranging between $20,000 and $30,000."*

*"I'd like to talk with you about the number of errors you've been making in figuring employee commissions. During the last pay period, we had to refigure commissions for five employees. Our accounting procedures need to be free of this type of error."*

Expressing empathy can be useful at this stage. You might begin by saying, "I understand that it can be difficult for you to . . . but I expect . . ."

*"Last week, I heard you shout at two different customers who came to you with complaints. I know some customers are difficult to deal with, but our associates are always expected to speak in a normal tone of voice."*

## Take a Moment

Using the employee you identified at the beginning of the book as a case example, describe the current behavior including the situation and the person's actions. Remember to be as specific as possible and focus on behavior, not attitude.

_____

_____

_____

_____

_____

# 3 Step

# Encourage Employee Self-Assessment

Before you continue with more detailed feedback, give the employee a chance to evaluate her or his own performance. Employees will be much more willing to participate actively in the coaching session if they have a chance to describe their own side of the situation. Hearing the employee's perspective will also help you determine what extenuating circumstances could be affecting his or her performance. It will give you a chance to verify those circumstances you might have noted earlier in your preparation process and to determine if coaching is really the best solution for the problem.

In order to help your employees express themselves during this part of the coaching session, you will need to develop two sets of skills:

- Questioning skills
- Active listening skills

## Questioning Skills

Some employees may be hesitant to offer their own ideas about their performance. One very effective way of getting people to open up is to ask open-ended questions—those that require more than a "yes" or "no" answer. Open-ended questions start with the words, "who," "what," "where," "when," "why," and "how." By asking questions that begin with . . .

*"What thoughts have you given to . . . ?"*

*"How does that fit into . . . ?"*

*"What is your understanding of . . . ?"*

. . . you will promote two-way collaborative communication.

Questions starting with "why" ("Why did you decide to . . . ?") should be used with caution because they risk coming across as challenging and may cause the other person to become defensive. On the other hand, questions that begin with "Tell me more about . . ." can encourage someone to expand his or her comments.

## Take a Moment

To help you with your own case study, make a list of open-ended questions you could ask your employee in order to unearth any underlying problems or extenuating circumstances. After you list your questions, brainstorm some possible explanations for performance problems your case employee might give you. (Of course, when you actually coach this individual, be aware that you might hear things you hadn't anticipated. Keep your mind open to other possibilities.)

_____

_____

_____

_____

_____

**To be fully effective, a coach's open-ended questions must be paired with active listening techniques.**

# Active Listening Skills

To be fully effective, a coach's open-ended questions must be paired with active listening techniques. Many managers fail in their coaching efforts because they spend most of their time in a coaching session talking. They tell the employee how to handle a situation differently instead of asking questions and really listening to the employee. This inability of managers to listen isn't surprising. Although listening constitutes 45 percent of our communication activity, most of us listen at only a 25-percent level of effectiveness.

## Listening Versus Hearing

Perhaps one reason why so many people are poor listeners is that they confuse listening with hearing. Hearing is the physical part of listening in which your ears sense sound waves. Listening, however, involves interpreting, evaluating, and reacting. Effective listening involves:

- Taking in information from the sender or speaker without judging.

- Clarifying what we think we heard.

- Responding to the speaker in a way that invites the communication to continue.

Coaches can develop a number of active listening techniques that will help them achieve these goals:

- Listen to the employee without allowing distractions to interfere.

- Clarify and confirm what the employee said.

- Reflect the employee's underlying feelings.

- Invite further contributions from the employee.

- Discuss the implications of the employee's statements.

- Probe to uncover the reasons why a situation exists and determine what should be done about it.

## Listen Without Distraction

When an employee speaks during a coaching session, give that person your undivided attention. Many things compete for our attention when we are listening. You may be distracted by noise from some other part of the office, or you may be trying to decide how you'll respond to the person's comments after he or she is finished. Block these from your mind and focus on what the other person is saying; you can determine your own response when he or she is done speaking. Show the other person that you're listening by maintaining eye contact while he or she speaks, and wait until the other person is done talking before you respond.

**Show the other person that you're listening by maintaining eye contact while he or she speaks, and wait until the other person is done talking before you respond.**

## Clarify and Confirm

When we listen, we interpret the speaker's message and then respond according to what we think he or she said. But often, our interpretations of that message are incorrect, and our responses can create misunderstandings and even conflict. It is important, therefore, to clarify what we think the speaker has just said by using some of the following approaches:

*"As I understand it, what you're saying is . . . "*

*"What I hear you saying is . . . "*

*"I get the impression that . . . "*

By paraphrasing the content of the message, the speaker can either confirm or further clarify the message, thus ensuring the accuracy of the communication.

## Reflect Underlying Feelings

Listen for attitudes, feelings, and motives behind the employee's words. Be alert to facial expressions, movements, gestures, and tone of voice. Confirm your perception by saying some of the following things:

**Listen for attitudes, feelings, and motives behind the employee's words.**

*"If that happened to me, I would be . . . "*

*"I can imagine that you must feel . . . "*

*"You sound upset about the situation. Let's talk more about . . . "*

*"I know that it's tough to sell when someone is watching, but . . . "*

## Invite Further Contribution

When employees give incomplete or short responses, the following will encourage them to expand on their points:

*"Tell me more about . . . "*

*"I would like to hear your thoughts about . . . "*

## Discuss Implications

Sometimes you may be clear on what the other person said but uncertain about the statement's full implications. Often this is a result of an incomplete message. To further clarify the speaker's intent, try to expand the discussion by using phrases similar to the following:

*"If you did that, then you would be able to . . . "*

*"Would that mean that . . . ?"*

### Probe to Uncover Reasons and Determine Next Steps

Asking more open-ended questions will help you discover the reasons behind an employee's behavior. Further probing will also help you lead the employee to ownership of the problem and a commitment to change. This type of questioning also supports the collaborative relationship:

*"What prompted you to . . . ?"*

*"How can I help you . . . ?"*

*"Where do you think we need to focus . . . ?"*

*"When would be the best time to . . . ?"*

*"Why do you think he/she responded . . . ?"*

Active listening is hard work, but it is well worth the effort. Active listening will result in more effective communication and more rewarding coaching relationships.

### Take a Moment

Visualize a coaching session with the employee you identified on page 14. What questions or statements could you use to promote two-way communication?

_____

_____

_____

_____

# Achieving Open Communication

If you successfully complete these opening steps of the coaching session, you and your employee will be able to engage in an open dialogue about the performance problem in question. In the next portion of the coaching session, you will build on this open communication to collaborate with the employee in generating a solution to the problem and an action plan for executing it.

# Chapter Four Review

Answers appear on pages 93 and 94.

1.  True or False?
    Coaching can be done any time, any place. Just pick a performance problem and jump in.

2.  When you describe a performance problem, you should state the problem in terms of
    _____ rather than _____ .

3.  True or False?
    Employees will be more willing to participate actively in a coaching session if they have a chance to describe their own perspective on the performance problem.

4.  What six words can be used to begin open-ended questions?
    _____
    _____
    _____
    _____
    _____
    _____

5.  Hearing is _____, while listening is _____ .

# Conducting the Coaching Session: Developing Solutions

## Chapter Objectives:

☑ Help the employee to acknowledge the nature of the performance problem and his or her role in it.

☑ Use indirect communication to encourage employee involvement in the coaching process.

☑ Join the employee in exploring alternative solutions to the problem.

☑ Use feedback to provide the employee with information that he or she can use to generate a solution to the problem. Agree on a solution to the problem.

In the remaining portion of the coaching session, you and the employee will work together to decide what should be done about the performance problem. To do this, you will need to complete the following steps:

■ **Step 4**—Agree on the nature of the problem and the employee's role in it.

■ **Step 5**—Explore alternative solutions.

■ **Step 6**—Agree on a solution to the problem.

# 4
## Step

# Agree on the Nature of the Problem

In order for coaching to be successful—and to determine whether it is needed at all—you and the employee must agree on the nature of the performance problem and the employee's role in it.

Some employees will already be aware of the problem and quickly agree with your initial description of it. But other employees may see the situation differently. They may not believe that a problem exists, or they may believe that other people are responsible for it. Give these employees the opportunity to express their views. Listen with an open mind. Do you agree with their assessment of the situation? If you do, then take it into account as the two of you try to solve the problem. Perhaps coaching isn't the best solution to this problem at all. If you are persuaded that the problem lies outside the employee, then this might be a good time to arrange for further training or some other option.

If you don't agree with the employee's view of the situation, you will need to provide more detailed feedback on performance to help the employee acknowledge the problem and take responsibility for it. The notes that you took during your observation of the employee's performance will be especially helpful if you need to convince an employee that he or she has a performance problem. Continue to describe what you have observed and discuss the situation with the employee until the two of you agree on the problem and the impact it has on the organization and others. You might also suggest that the employee ask him- or herself: "To what degree might I be contributing to the problem?" as in the following example:

*Raphael: Thanks for stopping by, Bradley. I'd like to discuss a problem I've been noticing with your performance. You were late getting your estimate figures to me on our last four jobs. We need to provide customers with estimates within 48 hours, or we'll lose business. When I don't get figures from you, it sets the whole process behind.*

*Bradley: I don't know what you're talking about. I do my job.*

> Some employees will already be aware of the problem and quickly agree with your initial description of it. But other employees may see the situation differently.

*Raphael:* You were a day late with the figures for the Costo and Jacobs jobs, and two days late with figures for the Cross and Kimball jobs.

*Bradley:* That wasn't my fault. It's the people in accounting. They just don't get me the numbers fast enough.

*Raphael:* The other estimators are able to get their estimates in on time, and they're working with the same accounting department. Can you think of anything you might be doing that could be contributing to the problem?

*Bradley:* I go in, I ask for the numbers. What else is there?

*Raphael:* Think about how you ask for the numbers. Do you give accounting all the information they need to process your request, or do they need to call you back with questions?

*Bradley:* Sometimes they have to call back.

*Raphael:* That could be adding to their time right there. What about deadlines? Do you clearly tell them when you need the figures?

*Bradley:* I shouldn't have to. They know we're on a tight schedule.

*Raphael:* They know time is tight, but it always helps to specify. Can you see now how you could be contributing to some of the lateness problems?

**Gaining agreement from your employee at this point in the coaching is critical to success.**

Gaining agreement from your employee at this point in the coaching is critical to success. For coaching to be effective, you and the employee must collaborate on a solution to the problem. The employee will have little motivation to participate in the coaching process if he or she believes that the problem doesn't exist or is someone else's responsibility.

## Take a Moment

What did Raphael do to help Bradley take responsibility for his performance problem?

_____
_____
_____
_____

Would the case study employee you identified on page 14 agree with your description of his or her performance problem? What do you think his or her response would be to your initial description of the problem?

_____
_____
_____
_____

If you don't think that the employee would agree that a problem exists, what would you say to convince him or her?

_____
_____
_____
_____

# Step 5

# Explore Alternative Solutions

**Remember that coaching is a collaborative process in which you and the employee must work together.**

After you and the employee have agreed on the nature of the problem, the two of you can explore solutions to it. As you begin this step, remember that coaching is a collaborative process in which you and the employee must work together. You should be able to do this if you continue your dialogue with the employee by:

■ Using indirect influence to encourage further participation and creative problem-solving from the employee.

■ Using feedback to provide the employee with more information regarding performance that could help him or her generate a solution.

# Encouraging Employee Participation

**In order to learn and grow, employees need to be active participants in the problem-solving process.**

As a coach, you may be tempted to use your *direct influence* with the employee and simply tell him or her how to solve the performance problem. However, this would do both you and the employee a disservice. In order to learn and grow, employees need to be active participants in the problem-solving process. Their involvement will lead to a better solution, which in turn will lead to better performance and improved productivity for your entire team.

Instead of directly telling employees what to do during the coaching session, you can encourage the initiative, independence, and self-expression necessary for successful collaboration through indirect influence. *Indirect influence* consists of four basic techniques:

- Accepting feelings.
- Developing ideas.
- Giving praise and encouragement.
- Asking open-ended questions.

## Accepting Feelings

**Employees must be able to express themselves during the coaching session.**

Employees may experience a variety of emotions during the coaching process. They may feel that they are being unfairly singled out or that management's expectations for them are unreasonable. In order to resolve these feelings and move toward a positive solution to the performance problem, they must be able to express themselves during the coaching session. Coaches can help by giving employees the opportunity to voice their feelings and accepting feelings that are expressed. Statements like, "I can imagine that what he said upset you," show employees that their feelings are accepted as legitimate and valid, as in the following example:

*Employee: Senior management has no idea what it's like to have a customer yelling at you when you're just trying to do your job.*

*Coach:*    *I know it can be stressful and frustrating when you're caught in the middle between company policy and satisfying the customer. Let's try to think of some approaches that will make these situations easier for you.*

## Developing Ideas

Employees may not only have strong feelings about a situation but also very definite ideas about what is taking place. In order to maintain open communication, you need to listen to the employee and help him or her clarify, build, and develop those ideas. This technique is similar to that used in active listening and involves such responses as, "Let me make sure I understand what you're saying," and "As I hear it, you're saying that. . . ."

At times, you may disagree with the ideas the employee expresses. However, you should still listen to and acknowledge them. The two of you can work out the differences as the discussion continues.

*Employee:*     *Some people are coming in late and leaving early, while the rest of us have to pick up the slack.*

*Coach:*     *So as I understand it, you're saying that some people aren't doing their fair share when it comes to opening and closing the store. Can you describe any specific situations when this has happened?*

## Giving Praise and Encouragement

Many employees lack confidence in their ideas and their ability to improve performance. By giving praise or encouragement, a coach can help an employee overcome this lack of confidence. Nonverbal gestures like nodding the head or simple comments like "go on" can help an employee see his or her ideas as worthwhile. Employees who lack faith in their own abilities may need more encouragement, as in the following example:

*Employee:*     *I'm having a hard time learning this new system.*

*Coach:*     *I know the new system is a challenge, but I'm sure you can do it. Remember, you learned the old system. It just takes some time to get used to a new way of doing things.*

## Asking Open-Ended Questions

Asking open-ended questions are as important at this point in the coaching process as they are at the beginning. Questions that begin with "who," "what," "when," "where," and "how" encourage the employee to develop his or her thoughts, which will lead the two of you to a more thorough, well-reasoned solution, as in the following.

| | |
|---|---|
| *Employee:* | *I don't think this plan will work.* |
| *Coach:* | *Let's talk about it more specifically. What aspect of it do you think is causing the problem?* |
| *Employee:* | *The shipping costs are way too high.* |
| *Coach:* | *OK, what are some alternative ways we could ship?* |

## Avoiding Negative Responses

Just as certain words and phrases encourage employees to speak freely, others discourage dialogue by conveying that the employee's opinion is not needed or valued. To support open, two-way communication throughout the coaching session, avoid these types of negative responses:

**Warnings:** *"If you don't. . . ."*

**Unsolicited advice:** *"You ought to. . . ."* or *"If I were you, I would. . . ."*

**Challenges:** *"Why did you. . . ?"*

**Patronizing:** *"You'll get over it."* or *"You'll be OK."*

**Devaluing experiences:** *"You think you have it bad? When that happened to me. . . ."*

**Devaluing emotions:** *"You shouldn't feel that way."*

## Helping Reluctant Employees

**The coaching session is most effective when the employee takes an active role in solving his or her own problem.**

Sometimes during coaching sessions, employees will insist that their managers provide them with a solution to a problem instead of generating one themselves. Remember, the coaching session is most effective when the employee takes an active role in solving his or her own problem. If an employee responds to your coaching efforts with "I'll do whatever you say," or "Tell me what to do," resist the temptation. Continue to ask open-ended questions that will encourage the employee to engage in the problem-solving process.

Use indirect influence to respond to the following statements an employee might make during a coaching session.

*Employee:*   *I don't know how management expects me to get any work done when I've got ten different people demanding things from me at the same time.*

*Coach:*

_____

_____

_____

*Employee:*   *The way I see it, the problem is that we've got some people in this shop who don't maintain their equipment properly.*

*Coach:*

_____

_____

_____

*Employee:*   *I don't think I'll ever be able to get this new software figured out.*

*Coach:*

_____

_____

_____

## Providing Detailed Feedback

**It's important for you to share any information you have that could help the employee.**

While it's important for you to encourage the employee to take an active role in solving the performance problem, it's just as important for you to share any information you have that could help the employee. In your observations, you probably noticed aspects of performance about which the employee is unaware.

Is the employee doing something that ruins sales or alienates coworkers without even knowing it? The only way that person can change that behavior is if you describe what you've observed. Did you notice a behavior that you'd like to see the employee repeat? Let him or her know—most people appreciate positive reinforcement.

**The reason for giving feedback is not to scold the employee for past mistakes, but to provide information that will help the employee succeed in the future.**

You may feel awkward about giving feedback to others, especially if you have received feedback that you thought was unfair or inappropriate. You can overcome your awkwardness if you remember that the reason for giving feedback is not to scold the employee for past mistakes, but to provide information that will help the employee succeed in the future. Never give critical feedback without also providing the opportunity to discuss how the performance can be improved, and don't focus solely on the negative. Practice catching people doing something right and telling them about it.

Both positive feedback and critical feedback need to be specific. Just telling someone that they're doing a good job or that they need to improve is not helpful. It is much more effective and meaningful to say something like, "John, I liked the way you handled that difficult customer. You showed a great deal of restraint and professionalism by not raising your voice or losing control."

## Feedback Guidelines

Your feedback will be more effective and useful if you keep the following guidelines in mind:

**Focus your feedback on behavior, not attitude.**

- *Focus on behavior, not attitude.* Focus your feedback on the behaviors you have observed, not on the attitudes you think an employee might hold. Instead of saying, "You never take your work seriously," try "Your last report contained several errors that needed to be reworked."

- *Be descriptive rather than evaluative.* Describe the behavior you have observed and its consequences without evaluating or passing judgment. Let the consequences speak for themselves: "When we have to rework errors, it makes the entire quarterly report late."

- *Be specific rather than general.* Describe behavior in the context of an actual situation: "I really liked the way you helped the confused guest we had on Tuesday morning. Your directions to her were clear and easy for her to follow, and you took the time to draw her a map."

- *Discuss only behavior the person can change.* Be sure that the employee is actually responsible for the behavior in question before you provide feedback on it.

- *Control your emotions and be sensitive to the employee's emotions.* Giving and receiving feedback can be an emotional process, especially if you or the employee are frustrated over the situation. Never raise your voice to an employee or react out of anger, no matter how strongly you feel. If the employee becomes upset, suggest that you take a break.

- *Communicate clearly.* Be sure that the employee's interpretation of your words is accurate by asking the person to state his or her understanding of the discussion. Don't simply ask, "Do you understand?" This type of question is patronizing, and the employee may answer "yes" out of confusion or embarrassment.

## Take a Moment

You have an employee who is always late, who turns in work that is filled with errors, and who frequently argues with clients and other employees. You are very frustrated with the situation. What feedback would you give this employee?

_____

_____

_____

_____

**Possible response**—Don't let your feelings of frustration influence what you say to the employee. Though the employee's actions suggest that he or she cares little about the job, focus on behaviors rather than the employee's internal motivation. Describe the situations you have observed and how they affect other people. Then ask the employee for his or her perspective. Keep describing the implications of the situation until the employee takes responsibility for correcting the problem.

## Helping Employees Receive Feedback

Receiving feedback graciously and nondefensively is as much a skill as giving it. You may need to give your employees some tips to help them receive feedback with an open mind:

■ Develop a positive attitude toward feedback. Look at feedback as an opportunity to collect important information that will help you become the person you wish to become.

■ Be prepared for feedback. Make sure that when you ask for feedback, you are ready to accept it, even if it's critical. If you don't think you can deal with feedback at this time, wait until you are capable of handling it.

■ Don't get defensive. It's human to become defensive when someone suggests we change our behavior. Remember, feedback represents one person's reaction to or perception of your performance. It has nothing to do with your overall abilities or your personal worth as an individual.

■ Check for understanding and clarification. Use active listening techniques, such as stating, "Let me make sure I understand what you're saying," and paraphrasing what you think you heard. If the person giving feedback describes something in general terms, ask for specific examples.

**Feedback is like a gift. And as with any gift, we thank the giver and then decide whether we want to keep it.**

Feedback is like a gift. And as with any gift, we thank the giver and then decide whether we want to keep it. Whenever you receive feedback, ask yourself if it has meaning and validity. Verify feedback by asking others if they share the same perceptions. You can collect different viewpoints, compare points of similarity and difference, and create a more objective picture of the situation. You can then use the information to either reinforce or modify your behavior accordingly.

# 6
## Step

# Agree on a Solution to the Problem

After you and the employee have discussed the performance problem and alternatives for solving it, you will need to agree on a specific solution. As the two of you collaborate, keep in mind that your solution must be realistic and workable in order to succeed. State your solution in terms of behaviors that the employee can perform and that you can observe and measure rather than in terms of attitude or emotions.

You can help your employee choose the best solution by:

■ Asking open-ended questions to help the employee identify possible barriers to enacting the solution. These can take the form of "What if. . . ?" questions:

*Employee:*      *I think I could improve my turnaround time on projects if the managers would give me a day's notice before they gave me work.*

*Coach:*      *What do you think would happen differently if you asked the managers to do that?*

■ Asking more questions to help the employee generate strategies for overcoming those barriers. These questions should encourage the employee to take a second look at situations:

*Employee:*      *I know I could meet deadlines if I knew how to use the software better, but with three people sharing a computer, I never get a chance to practice.*

*Coach:*      *Is there another computer in the office you might be able to use a few times until you're up to speed?*

As you work with the employee, you should also ask what you can do to help him or her make the solution a success. It may not be appropriate or possible for you to do everything the employee asks; if that's the case, it's a good starting point for further discussion and negotiation. The employee may even generate a better solution during your dialogue.

# Role-Playing

As you and the employee work toward agreement on a solution, role-playing can provide a helpful tool. Role-playing can serve a variety of uses at this point in the coaching session, including:

■ Helping the employee see the effects of various solutions.

■ Giving the employee a chance to practice new behaviors and actions.

**As you work with the employee, you should also ask what you can do to help him or her make the solution a success.**

The following scenario illustrates how role-playing can be used in both ways:

*Salome is coaching Ron on how to handle irate customers. The two of them have generated a number of alternatives and are now trying to choose the best approach. Salome takes the role of customer service representative and acts out the various approaches. Ron, playing the customer, predicts the response. Once the two of them have identified the most effective approach, they switch roles. This gives Ron the chance to practice the approach before meeting actual customers.*

# Case Study 1: The Sales Call

As you read the following dialogue, ask yourself whether the sales manager is using the effective coaching techniques we've discussed so far. Are there things you would try to do differently if you were the coach?

*Scenario:* Roberta, a sales manager in a pharmaceutical company, has accompanied Sam, a new sales representative, on his sales calls. The two have called on four physicians that morning and five in the afternoon. It's near the end of the day, and the sales manager suggests that they stop at a coffee shop for a debriefing session before they call it a day.

*Roberta:* It's been a pretty exhausting afternoon, hasn't it?

*Sam:*  Boy, I'll say! Some of these doctors can be really tough to sell to.

*Roberta:* Well, that's what I want to talk to you about. I thought this would be a good opportunity to give you some feedback on what I observed and also give you some suggestions to help your calls go more smoothly. After all, both your goal and mine is to help you make more sales. Right?

*Sam:*  Absolutely. Okay, let me have it.

*Roberta:* Let me start by saying that I think one of your biggest assets is that you are very warm and friendly. That really helps in establishing rapport with the customer. You have a great personality, and you do a great job of connecting with the doctors.

**I thought this would be a good opportunity to give you some feedback on what I observed and also give you some suggestions to help your calls go more smoothly.**

**Sam:** That's good to know. I've been told that I have the gift of gab and can sell anything to anybody.

**Roberta:** You certainly have the talent. All we need to do now is to fine-tune those skills. One of the things you have going for you is that you seem to know the products well. It's obvious that you're well-versed on the features and benefits of each product. You do a good job of getting the main points across in a very limited amount of time. Do you agree?

**Sam:** Absolutely. I'm really confident that I know the products.

The biggest thing I notice is that in your eagerness and enthusiasm, you aren't taking enough time to plan your sales call.

**Roberta:** Since product knowledge is not a problem, we need to take a look at what is getting in the way of a really successful sales call. The biggest thing I notice is that in your eagerness and enthusiasm, you aren't taking enough time to plan your sales call. As a result, you come across as disorganized and unprepared. That's one thing. The second problem I see is that you seem to be a little too eager to close the sale based on one or two of the physician's needs instead of taking the time to analyze the situation. Do you know what I mean?

**Sam:** I'm not sure I do.

What I would recommend for your next set of calls is to do a better job of planning, including the preparation of some open probes.

**Roberta:** For one thing, you don't ask enough open-ended questions to uncover what the physician's most important needs really are. Because you know the products so well, you seem to focus on just telling the doctor about the products. I also think that you need to do a better job of really listening to what the doctor is telling you. I don't think you're picking up on the nonverbal cues. What I would recommend for your next set of calls is to do a better job of planning, including the preparation of some open probes. During the call, concentrate on asking open-ended questions and really paying attention to the doctor's responses, including body language. Other than those few things, I think you're doing a good job. So, do you think you can work on these things?

**Sam:** Well . . . OK.

**Roberta:** Good. I'm sure you'll see a big difference the next time out.

## Take a Moment

Take a moment now to jot down those things you thought the coach did well and those areas in which you think she could improve.

What did the coach do well?

_____

_____

_____

_____

What could the coach have done better?

_____

_____

_____

_____

**Here are some features you might have listed:**

*What the coach did well*—By accompanying Sam on sales calls, Roberta was able to observe his performance. She analyzed what he was doing and compared it to her expectations for him. She took the time to build rapport at the beginning of the coaching session and to point out aspects of Sam's performance that were effective as well as those things she hoped he would change.

*What the coach could have done better*—Roberta identified two performance problems for Sam: that he appeared "disorganized and unprepared" and that he needed to focus more on the doctors' needs instead of just describing the product. Her description of the first problem was too general to be useful. Instead of calling Sam disorganized, she should have described specific incidents from the sales calls: "In one call, you forgot the doctor's name, and in another, you were confused about the doctor's specialty." She also didn't provide an opportunity to discuss how Sam might solve this first performance problem.

Roberta provided more detail in her description of Sam's second performance problem, but she didn't give Sam much opportunity for self-assessment. He was never able to say whether he agreed with her view of his performance or not. He also didn't get much of an opportunity to ask questions about Roberta's feedback.

**Instead of calling Sam disorganized, Roberta should have described specific incidents from the sales calls.**

**Roberta provided Sam with advice instead of allowing him to generate ideas for solutions.**

Roberta provided Sam with advice instead of allowing him to generate ideas for solutions. She did not even take the time to see that he fully understood her advice. Sam's statements "I don't know what you mean" and "I guess so" show his confusion, but she didn't pick up on it and offer him any further explanation. Roberta also didn't ask Sam any questions to determine whether her solution to the situation was really the best one. Sam really wasn't a full partner in this coaching session, and he will probably have some difficulty enacting the changes that Roberta recommended.

Here are some different approaches Roberta could have taken when describing Sam's performance problems:

Roberta: *One thing I noticed during your sales calls is that you sometimes got confused when you were talking to the doctors. In one call, you forgot the doctor's name and in another call, you were confused about the doctor's specialty. That type of thing can make the doctors feel that they aren't important to you. What do you think might be happening here?*

Sam: *I try to plan out all my calls before I make them, but sometimes I get so excited that I forget to look at my notes before I go into the office. I need to slow down and review my notes before I get out of the car.*

Roberta: *That sounds like a good plan. Another thing I noticed is that you might be closing some of your calls too quickly instead of seeing if the doctors have other needs we can fill. Did you notice that both Dr. Cochran and Dr. Giddings seemed interested when you mentioned that we were putting our hay fever medication in liquid form?*

Sam: *No, I didn't. How could you tell?*

Roberta: *I watched their body language. Both of them leaned forward in their chairs and made direct eye contact when you started talking about the medication.*

*Sam:*     *If I'd noticed that, I could have signed them up for samples. I wish I knew more about body language. I'd pay more attention if I knew what to look for.*

*Roberta:*  *I have a book that might help you. I'll give it to you when we get back to the office.*

By engaging in open dialogue, Roberta and Sam were able to collaborate on solutions to Sam's performance problems. The solutions were more effective than the ones Roberta developed without input from Sam, and Sam will be more motivated to follow through on a solution that he helped develop. The final phase in this or any coaching session is to get the employee's commitment to a specific action plan to carry out the solution and to set up follow-up sessions to monitor the employee's progress.

# Chapter Five Review

Answers may be found on page 94.

1.  If you and the employee you are coaching do not agree on the
    nature of the performance problem and the employee's role in it,
    you should (choose one)
    a. Give the employee the opportunity to express his or her views.
    b. Refuse to compromise your authority by listening to any of the
       employee's arguments.

2.  Indirect influence consists of these four basic techniques:

    _____

    _____

    _____

    _____

3.  True or False?
    When providing feedback, you should describe what employees
    are doing right as well as what they need to improve.

4.  List four of the six guidelines for giving effective feedback.

    _____

    _____

    _____

    _____

5.  What are two techniques you can use during a coaching session to
    help an employee choose the best solution to a problem?

    _____

    _____

# Action-Planning and Follow-Up

## Chapter Objectives:

☑ Help the employee develop an action plan for improving performance.

☑ Monitor the employee's performance as he or she works to improve.

☑ Provide follow-up coaching as needed.

The final phase of the coaching process involves:

■ **Step 1**—Creating an action plan to put the solution you have agreed on into action.

■ **Step 2**—Monitoring the employee's progress.

■ **Step 3**—Scheduling and conducting follow-up coaching sessions as needed.

## 1 Step Create an Action Plan

Once you and the employee have agreed on a workable solution, ask the employee to outline a plan for putting the solution into action. Then ask the employee to state it verbally. Developing an action plan will not only give the employee direction for making the solution a reality, but it will also help build employee commitment to seeing the solution work. The plan can be simple, as in the example on the following page.

*Coach:* We've talked about some different ways you can avoid word-processing errors. Could you review them for me?

*Employee:* I'll spell-check every document I type and read over each finished document to be sure I didn't leave anything out.

Of course, many actions plans will be more detailed than the above example. In these cases, ask the employee to spell out deadlines for performing various actions and what the end result will be:

*Coach:* Let's review exactly what you're going to do to get the quarterly report out on time and when you'll complete each step.

*Employee:* I'll ask accounting for the figures I need two weeks before the report is due, and I'll give them a one-week deadline. I'll call the department heads at the same time and ask if I can have their reports in one week. That should give me a full week to work with those materials before the final report is due.

**You can use your questioning and feedback skills to help the employee consider any obstacles that might keep the plan from succeeding.**

As in previous steps in the coaching process, you can use your questioning and feedback skills to help the employee consider any obstacles that might keep the plan from succeeding. If you have agreed to do something to support the employee's efforts, you should restate that as well:

*Coach:* I'll let each of the department heads know how important it is to get the material to you on time.

# 2 Step  3 Step

# Monitor Employee Progress and Provide Follow-Up

After you and the employee have agreed on an action plan, the two of you should set up a time when you can meet and discuss the employee's progress. This will give you the opportunity to monitor the employee and provide any follow-up coaching that might be necessary. Schedule your follow-up far enough in the future that the employee will have time to put the solution into practice but not so far off that he or she will begin to think that you've forgotten about the matter.

# Preparing for Follow-Up

To prepare for your follow-up session, observe the employee's performance. Is the employee successfully making the changes that the two of you agreed on? Are there performance areas that could still use improvement?

**Make note of what you observe, both the behaviors you want to reinforce and the behaviors that need further improvement.**

Make note of what you observe, both the behaviors you want to reinforce and the behaviors that need further improvement. Record specific examples of each that you can share with the employee during a follow-up session.

# Follow-Up Coaching

**Coaching is an ongoing process in which you and the employee will strive for continual improvement.**

Coaching is an ongoing process in which you and the employee will strive for continual improvement. Like your original coaching session, your follow-up coaching session will give you a chance to provide your employee with feedback on what you've observed about the employee's performance and give the employee a chance to describe any barriers he or she may have encountered. Based on this information, you may continue to revise your solution until both you and the employee are satisfied that the problem is solved.

You can also provide your employee with informal follow-up coaching as you observe his or her performance. Informal follow-up coaching is most effective if done immediately after you have observed the behavior in question. For example, if you saw an employee handle a difficult customer successfully, you might wait until the customer left and then say, "You handled that customer well. Even though you couldn't give her what she wanted, you gave her a choice and let her make her own decision." Remember never to let informal coaching turn into a situation in which you take over and perform the employee's job. Even if the employee is having difficulty, wait until the situation is over before you offer advice.

## Take a Moment

Using the employee you identified on page 14 as an example, write down some ways you could monitor the employee's progress. Remember, however, you are doing this in isolation. In the actual situation, the employee would help determine the appropriate plan of action.

_____

_____

_____

_____

# Case Study 2: Hold the Phone

By now you should be familiar with all the steps of the coaching process. Can you identify them in action? Read the following discussion between a manager and an employee. Then identify the steps the manager follows to coach the employee to improve performance. At the end, you'll have a chance to evaluate the manager's coaching abilities and describe what you would have done differently.

*Scenario:* Chris, a store manager, must help Robin, a sales associate, come up with a better way to handle phone calls when customers are in the store.

Chris: *Robin, come in and have a seat. I'd like to talk to you about a problem I've been noticing with your job performance.*

Robin: *What are you talking about? I've been doing my job OK.*

Chris: *Yes, Robin, you perform your job duties very well. However, I want to talk with you about your interactions with the customers on the telephone. On six different occasions during the past two weeks, I've noticed that you allowed the telephone to ring at least six times before you answered it. When you finally did answer it, you told the callers to wait a minute. Then when you got back to the customers on the phone, you asked them what they wanted and didn't apologize for keeping them waiting. I have noticed this behavior on several occasions. What seems to be the problem from your perspective?*

Robin: *I don't think there is a problem. I get back to them as soon as I can. After all, there's only one of me, and I often have other customers in front of me that I have to take care of. What do you want me to do—ignore them?*

Chris: *As we have discussed in our training sessions and staff meetings, we are committed to providing the highest level of customer service to all of our customers, both face-to-face and on the telephone.*

Robin: *Look, I'm doing the best I can. Maybe if you hired more people we wouldn't have this problem. I can't do two things at the same time. Besides, if they don't want to hold, they can call back later. And I'm not the only one who doesn't answer the phone right away, but I don't notice you giving anybody else grief. Have you talked to John about it? He never answers the phone unless he has to.*

**Let's keep in mind that we expect everyone to provide the best service to our customers.**

Chris: *Let's keep in mind that we expect everyone to provide the best service to our customers. And right now, we're talking about your performance. I understand that at times you are pulled in several directions at the same time. I did say that the customer in front of you should take priority; however, the customer on the telephone can't see that you have a customer in front of you, and when the telephone rings and rings, the caller gets frustrated and angry.*

Robin: *So what do you want me to do?*

Chris: *Robin, what do you think you could do to keep the customer in front of you happy while responding to the incoming call?*

Robin: *I don't know. That's what I'm asking you.*

**Chris:** I suggest that you ask the customer in front of you to excuse you for a moment and then immediately answer the telephone. Then ask the caller if you can put him or her on hold, or if he or she would like you to call back when you're free.

**Robin:** That's what I do now. I tell 'em to hold.

**Chris:** Robin, there's a difference between telling someone to hold and asking if he or she would like to hold.

**Robin:** What difference does it make? Nobody likes to be put on hold, so why bother asking?

**Chris:** People like to be given options. They like to feel that they are making the decision.

**Robin:** Okay, fine. I'll do it. Is there anything else?

**Chris:** Not really. Let's just make sure we're both clear on the action plan. Tell me what you are going to do differently in dealing with the customers.

**Robin:** I'm going to concentrate on answering the phone more promptly. And I will be friendlier and apologize for putting the customer on hold.

**Chris:** Good. Let's get together again in two weeks to discuss how things are going. How does that sound to you?

**Robin:** Okay, I guess. I'll give it a try.

## Take a Moment

Identify the various steps of the coaching process that you see in this interaction. (If you need a review, turn to the flowchart on page 35.)

Once you've identified the steps of the coaching process, make a note of those steps that you thought the coach executed well and those areas in which you thought the coach could improve.

What did the coach do well?

_____

_____

_____

_____

What could the coach improve upon?

_____

_____

_____

_____

*Here are some features you might have noticed:*

*What the coach did well*—Chris did a good job of describing Robin's current performance with the telephone and citing specific incidents when Robin left customers on hold. Chris invited Robin's self-assessment of the problem and kept Robin on the topic when Robin wanted to talk about other employees and their performance problems.

Chris empathized with Robin's difficulty with being pulled in several different directions at once when dealing with customers in person and on the phone, yet Chris did not buy into Robin's complaint that more employees were needed. Chris made sure that Robin clarified an action plan for improving performance and stated exactly what the plan would involve. Chris also set up a follow-up time for monitoring Robin's performance.

*What the coach could have done better*—Chris didn't take time to build rapport with Robin at the beginning of the coaching session, and the

**Chris didn't take time to build rapport with Robin at the beginning of the coaching session.**

abrupt mentioning of the performance problem put Robin on the defensive. Chris might have received more cooperation from Robin by opening the coaching session this way:

Chris: Hi, Robin, could you come in here a minute. How are things going for you on the sales floor?

Robin: Fine, I guess. We've been really busy lately.

Chris: I've noticed that. I've also noticed that we've been getting a lot of phone calls while customers are in the store. I know it's difficult to juggle the phone when you have people in front of you. So I wanted to talk about some ways you could do that more effectively.

Chris also wasn't assertive enough in getting Robin to generate a solution to the problem. Though the two of them agreed on a solution, Robin had no part in creating it and may not be motivated to make the behavioral changes to carry it out. Chris might have gotten more involvement from Robin by encouraging Robin to think of the situation from a customer's perspective.

**Chris might have gotten more involvement from Robin by encouraging Robin to think of the situation from a customer's perspective.**

Chris: Robin, what do you think you could do to keep the customer in front of you happy while responding to the incoming call?

Robin: I don't know. That's what I'm asking you.

Chris: Put yourself in the customer's place. You've called places before and been put on hold. How does it make you feel?

Robin: I hate it. No one likes to be put on hold.

Chris: OK, so you don't like it. Why not?

Robin: It's a waste of time. You never know how long you're going to wait before someone can talk to you.

Chris: What could the people on the other end do to make it easier on you?

Robin: Tell me how long it's going to take, for one thing.

Chris: What if we tried that with our customers?

**Through coaching, you can actively involve employees in the problem-solving process and encourage them to take responsibility for their own professional development and success on the job.**

# Successful Coaching, Step-by-Step

We have seen that, by following the steps of the coaching process, you can help your employees improve their performance. Through coaching, you can actively involve employees in the problem-solving process and encourage them to take responsibility for their own professional development and success on the job. This will not only improve productivity but will also build job satisfaction and motivation as your employees begin to participate in decisions that affect their job performance.

Coaching is the management technique of the future, and the sooner you begin to develop your coaching skills, the better. In the final chapter, you'll have the chance to create an action plan for putting the techniques you've learned in this book into practice.

# Chapter Six Review

Answers may be found on pages 94 and 95.

1. Creating an action plan can (circle one)
   a. Give an employee direction for making the agreed-on solution a reality.
   b. Build employee commitment to seeing the solution work.
   c. Both.

2. What can a coach do to prepare for a follow-up session with an employee?

   _____

   _____

   _____

   _____

3. A follow-up session gives the coach a chance to

   _____

   and gives the employee a chance to

   _____

4. Follow-up coaching can be
   a. Formal.
   b. Informal.
   c. Both.

# Developing a Personal Action Plan

## Chapter Objectives:

☑ Overcome obstacles to coaching.

☑ Evaluate your readiness to coach.

☑ Develop a plan for improving your coaching skills.

☑ Monitor and evaluate your success as a coach.

# Preventing Coaching Pitfalls

**The effort you put into developing your coaching skills will be richly rewarded.**

There's no doubt that coaching takes time, patience, and practice. But the effort you put into developing your coaching skills will be richly rewarded. Coaching gets results. The organization benefits from improved employee performance, increased productivity and bottom-line results. The employee benefits from increased self-esteem and job satisfaction. The manager benefits by meeting goals and objectives with less stress.

As you begin to develop your coaching skills, you may find barriers to coaching within your organization. You may be one of the few people in your organization who is willing to take the time to coach. You may even work in an organization that does not reward or value coaching as a management practice. But don't give up. Effective coaching can only improve the performance of your team or department, and when other managers see its effectiveness, you'll be on the way to creating a coaching culture within your organization.

Employees themselves may initially resist coaching. Those who have never been given the opportunity to participate in decisions or use their own judgment may be suspicious and need reassurance that your efforts are sincere. Emphasize that you are trying to help your employees reach their full potential and that each one is responsible for his or her own professional growth and development.

# Your Action Plan for Coaching

How will you develop your coaching skills? Just as you would require an employee to develop an action plan to improve performance, use this opportunity to create one for yourself by answering the following questions:

■ To improve my coaching skills, I plan to

_____

_____

_____

■ Action steps I will take to improve my coaching skills include

_____

_____

_____

■ Obstacles that may hinder my efforts to become an effective coach include

_____

_____

_____

■ Steps I will take to overcome obstacles include

_____

_____

_____

■ I will know I have succeeded in becoming a more successful coach when

_____

_____

_____

# Measuring Success

One of the ways you can measure your coaching success is to solicit feedback from your employees. One easy and relatively risk-free method is to ask each employee to complete an anonymous "agree-disagree" questionnaire, as in the following example:

| Please indicate whether you agree or disagree with each statement. Please express your true feelings—your responses will remain anonymous. | Agree | Disagree |
|---|---|---|
| **My manager** <br> 1. Frequently tells me how I'm doing. | | |
| 2. Gives me both positive and negative feedback. | | |
| 3. Tells me what he/she expects of me. | | |
| 4. Asks my opinion and involves me in decisions that affect me. | | |
| 5. Keeps me informed about changes taking place in the organization. | | |
| 6. Does not use threats or intimidation. | | |
| 7. Acknowledges my extra effort with some type of praise or recognition. | | |
| 8. Takes the time to explain new procedures and makes sure I understand. | | |
| 9. Provides the training and resources I need to do my job. | | |
| 10. Treats me with respect. | | |
| 11. Is not afraid to admit his/her mistakes or to say, "I'm sorry." | | |

Respond to the list on the previous page as you think your employees would respond. Are there any areas you would like to improve? Compare your self-perception with the perception of your employees—it could be a real eye-opener! Regardless of the outcome, you now have valuable data that reinforces the positive approach you are already using for identifying areas for improvement.

Effective coaching takes time, effort, and a real interest in and commitment to developing people. The investment is substantial, but the payoff is enormous.

# Final Review

Review your understanding of the coaching process by answering the following statements. Answers appear on page 95.

1. True or False?
   In a coaching session, the coach should speak for the majority of the time.

2. True or False?
   One of the most effective ways to encourage two-way communication is to ask open-ended questions.

3. True or False?
   One of the coach's responsibilities is to help employees solve their own problems.

4. True or False?
   Coaching sessions should always be spontaneous and unstructured.

5. True or False?
   Every coaching session should end with both parties agreeing on an action plan.

6. True or False?
   The purpose of coaching is to correct behavior.

7. True or False?
   During the coaching session, the coach should refrain from overloading the employee with too many points.

8. True or False?
   Performance appraisal time is usually the best occasion for coaching.

9. True or False?
   *Coaching* and *counseling* mean the same thing.

10. True or False?
    Coaching is an ongoing process.

# Answers to Chapter Reviews

## Chapter One

1.  False—An annual performance appraisal cannot take the place of regular coaching.

2.  Chronic tardiness or absenteeism—c. Provide counseling
    Meeting only minimum standards—a. Provide coaching
    New responsibilities—b. Provide training

3.  They don't know how to coach.
    They don't want to take time to coach.
    They don't have the patience to coach.
    They believe employees should improve performance on their own.

4.  They are resistant to change.
    They think they know it all.

5.  b. Placing results above all other concerns is not a characteristic of a good coach.

6.  Choose from communicating effectively, listening, questioning, setting goals and objectives, establishing appropriate priorities, analyzing, planning and organizing.

## Chapter Two

1.  Maintainers—Choose from working conditions, company policies, job security, pay and benefits, relationships, supervision, and status.
    Motivators—Choose from achievement, recognition, satisfying work, responsibility, advancement, growth.

2.  True—Employees ranked the feeling of *being in on things* as one of the top three things they wanted from their jobs.

3. False—Younger workers want different things than their parents or grandparents did from their jobs. Younger workers are interested in rewarding challenges and are willing to work hard. But unlike their parents, they fiercely guard their personal and leisure time.

4. Expect the best from employees.
Develop a flexible management style.
Eliminate barriers to individual achievement.

5. True—Different employees require different types of rewards and recognition.

## Chapter Three

1. a. At the beginning of the coaching process, before the coaching session begins.

2. Specific behaviors that can be measured and changed.
What the employee is doing right as well as things that need to be improved.
The priority of the behaviors that the employee needs to improve.

3. Choose from lack of proper training, too few resources, unrealistic parameters, too many other responsibilities.

4. Candid—d. Direct and controlling; likes to be the center of attention.
Persuasive—b. Outgoing, warm, and animated.
Logical—a. Uses analysis and reason in all situations.
Reflective—c. Reliable and cautious; seeks security and avoids conflict.

## Chapter Four

1. False—Coaching should only be done after the proper coaching environment has been created.

2. When you describe a performance problem, you should state the problem in terms of behaviors rather than the employee's attitude or emotional state.

3. True—Employees will be more willing to participate actively in a coaching session if they have a chance to describe their own perspective on the performance problem.

4. Who, what, where, when, why, and how.

5. Hearing is the physical part of listening in which your ears sense sound waves. Listening is interpreting, evaluating, and reacting.

## Chapter Five

1. a. Give the employee the opportunity to express his or her views.

2. Accepting feelings.
   Developing ideas.
   Giving praise and encouragement.
   Asking open-ended questions.

3. True—When providing feedback, you should describe what employees are doing right as well as what they need to improve.

4. Choose from:
   Focus on behavior, not attitude.
   Be descriptive rather than evaluative.
   Be specific rather than general.
   Discuss only behavior the person can change.
   Control your emotions and be sensitive to the employee's emotions.
   Communicate clearly.

5. Ask open-ended questions to help the employee identify possible barriers to enacting the solution. Ask more questions to help the employee generate strategies for overcoming those barriers.

## Chapter Six

1. c. Both: Creating an action plan can give an employee direction for making the agreed-on solution a reality and build employee commitment to seeing the solution work.

2. Observe the employee's performance.
   Make note of what you observe.

3. A follow-up session gives the coach a chance to provide feedback on what he or she has observed about the employee's performance and gives the employee a chance to describe any barriers he or she may have encountered in trying to improve performance.

4. c. Follow-up coaching can be both formal and informal.

## Final Review

Answers to Coaching Process True-False statements:

| | |
|---|---|
| 1. F | 6. F |
| 2. T | 7. T |
| 3. T | 8. F |
| 4. F | 9. F |
| 5. T | 10. T |